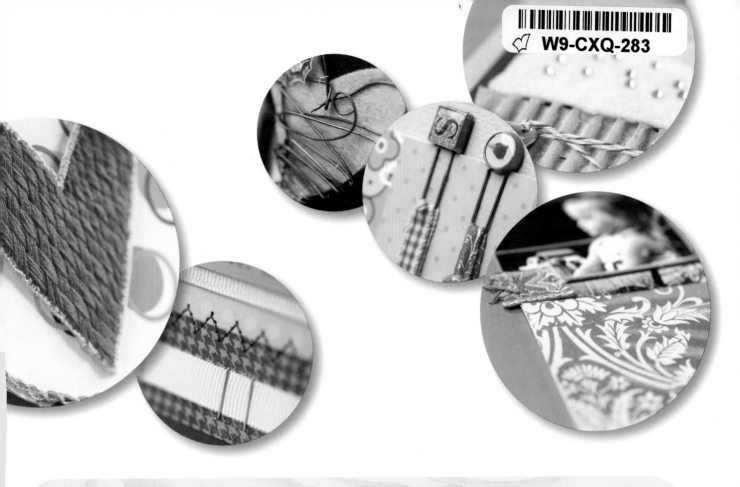

WELCOME

What makes you "ohhh" and "ahhh" over a baby girl outfit? Is it because it's pink? Probably not. It's most likely the little scallops that adorn the edge of the sleeve or the flowers down the bodice. At a wedding, it's the little details like the favors lovingly placed next to each place setting that make the night so memorable. And in a home, candles burning, flames flickering in the fireplace and a welcome basket in the guest room can make a guest feel special and remembered. Summer Baltzer from the show *Design on a Dime* said it best: "The design is in the details." The details and finishing touches on a room, event or project are what make them feel complete and personalized.

Designing With Details will take your pages from ordinary to extraordinary as you learn how to pay special attention to details. By adding those irresistible touches to your work, you can masterfully communicate the message and meaning behind your art. Get out your designer's notebook and make notes that will help you complete and personalize your projects.

ASHLEY CALDER

CANDICE CARPENTER

LISA RUSSO

THE
ARTISTS
of Autumn Leaves

CATHY BLACKSTONE

DANIELLE THOMPSON

JACKIE BONETTE

JAMIE WATERS

JENNIFER MCGUIRE

KELLI CROWE

LESLIE LIGHTFOOT

MARGIE SCHERSCHLIGT

MARILYN HEALEY

MELLETTE BEREZOSKI

PATRICIA ANDERSON

RENEE CAMACHO

RHONDA BONIFAY

ROBYN WERLICH

*Gillian Nelson photo not available

CONTENTS

HANDMADE

Why does discovering a handmade relic made by your grandma make your heart leap? Or why does touching a delicate doily your mom crocheted make you happy? Because it's handmade, that's why. There is something special about things that are handmade. Maybe it is the time taken to make the piece or the love that went into creating it; either way, handmade items tie your heart to the person who made it. When you include handmade accents on your projects, you can achieve the same personal touch as something your grandmother crafted and create details that will be treasured for generations.

CHRISTMAS MORNING

By Leslie

CUT PAPER accents and back with thin chipboard. Add paper, string and fabric embellishments. Hand stitch to give a handmade feel. Adhere at the bottom to create a border. Cut photos into circles and affix to layout.

Font: Kartika ● **Paper:** K&Co., 7gypsies, Anna Griffin, MAMBI, AL and SW ● **Photo corners:** Advantus

LOVE ME

By Jennifer

Cut felt shapes. Stitch to larger piece of felt to make a felt pillow. Cut title letters from felt and secure to layout.

Letters: Hobby Lobby ● **Font:** Franklin Gothic Book

NO TWO TREES

By Rhonda

Attach photo to right side of page. Cut a border with decorative scissors and adhere to the top and bottom of layout. Cut a tree from burlap and cut flowers, bird and leaves from fabric. Adhere to layout and hand stitch around the bird. Stitch buttons to centers of flowers. Punch small holes on upper and lower side of layout; weave with twine.

THE BOUGHS OF NO TWO TREES EVER HAVE THE SAME ARRANGEMENT. NATURE ALWAYS PRODUCES INDIVIDUALS.

— *Lydia Maria Child*

Boston November 2005

Fonts: AL Old Remington and Blackjack

SO HAPPY

By Jamie

MAT PHOTO on patterned paper. Tear patterned paper strip to go across the bottom. Cut shapes from plastic. Adhere with various embellishments. Apply rub-ons and hand write journaling.

Conchos: Scrapworks
Flowers: Prima
Paper: KI and AL
Rub-ons and buttons: AL
Stamps: Hero Arts
Stickers: KI and 7gypsies

so happy

to be a wife, mother, friend, scrapbooker. My days are filled with so much goodness

A GREAT THING By Renee

Buttons: AL
Chipboard: Pressed Petals
Foam: Fibre Craft
Fonts: AL Highlight
Paper: K&Co.
Sequins: Westrim Crafts

Stamp or add rub-ons to patterned and solid papers. Add fill-in detail with colored pencils. Punch hearts from embellished papers, adding decorative scissor trimming to some edges. Cover each piece with several layers of Diamond Glaze to create epoxy accents. Attach title letters and journaling strips to layout along with additional accent pieces.

3 YEARS OLDER By Patricia

PRINT TITLE and swirl design in reverse. Cut out and adhere to back of foam paper; cut along design. Cut diamond shapes and photo corner from foam paper. Make background from strips of cardstock. Adhere photos along with foam shapes. Finish page with buttons for accents.

Buttons: AL • **Chipboard:** Pressed Petals • **Foam:** Fibre Craft
Fonts: AL Highlight • **Paper:** K&Co. • **Sequins:** Westrim Crafts

there's
some
serious
goin' on

COZY

Apple & Blackjack

MAR 1 1 2006

SOME SERIOUS COZY

By Gillian

Knit small lengths of yarn and use as a page border or as a flower stem. Attach knitted strips by machine sewing over top.

Buttons and tags: MM • **Chipboard letters:** Li'l Davis • **Brad:** Junkitz • **Pen:** Marvy Uchida • **Yarn:** Hart

Apple & Blackjack

CHRISTMAS SEASON By Mellette

Beads and super tacky tape: Magic Scraps • **Fonts:** Chopin Script • **Frame and label holder:** Nunn Designs • **Page pebble and brads:** MM • **Paper:** Anna Griffin, MM and 7gypsies • **Rub-ons:** AL and MM

Cut chipboard into holly leaves and berries. Glue tissue paper to holly leaves. Machine stitch around edges and middle of leaves. Apply super tacky tape to round holly berries. Pour red beads over tape and shake off excess.

WHEN YOU TURNED ELEVEN

By Marilyn

ARRANGE LETTER forms on the computer and print out. Use it as a pattern for cutting the negative shapes from a thin balsa wood sheet. Paint the wood with acrylic paint. Assemble the wood onto rust cardstock, using the print out as a guide. Fill in the remaining open spaces with various patterned papers.

Fonts: Typewriter • **Paper:** KI • **Stamps:** Stampin' Up! and Purple Onion Designs • **Tags:** Collage Joy

By Ashley

IF I COULD

Hinge: MM ● **Paper:** AL, Scrapworks and DMD ● **Ribbon:** Li'l Davis ● **Stamps:** Purple Onion

Hand stitch flower stems onto orange felt; add paper flowers and additional stitching details. Mat photo on patterned paper; stitch corners using a variety of simple stitches. Back felt with yellow cardstock and add two additional photos. Blanket stitch around edge of layout. Using plait stitch, create heart on fabric and blanket stitch around edges. Adhere to paper with chain stitch around border and add to cover of mini book that contains journaling.

USING DIFFERENT gauges of wire, wrap the wire around a jar or cup that is the same size as punched paper circles. Vary how many times you wrap the wire (two times for thick wire, 10 times for really thin wire). Cut and loop the ends around the wire to hold the shape in place. Sew to page in three different locations on top of die cut circle cardstock shapes.

By Robyn SUNSHINE

Chipboard letter: Daisy Hill ● **Die cut:** Quickutz ● **Font:** AL Uncle Charles ● **Paper:** KI ● **Stencils and button:** AL

OAKS

By Kelli

Font: AL Uncle Charles
Paper: KI, AL, Paper Loft, MM and Paper Heart Studio

Tear paper into small rectangles; ink edges. Cover background with pieces using decoupage medium as the adhesive. For the tree, cut out shape from cardstock. Adhere rectangles to cut out and mount on layout with pop dots. Add gold foil accents. Hand stitch over the tree to accent.

THE REASONS WHY

By Jackie

Make a small quilted background by sewing together 2 ¾" squares of fabric with a ¼" seam allowance. Attach to the cardstock and then add other page elements on top of quilt.

Buttons: AL
Chipboard: MM
Font: 2Peas Teen
Ribbon: May Arts and Michaels
Stickers: AC and KI

WONDER

STAMP IMAGES or trace clipart onto shrink plastic and shrink. Use as page accents.

Fonts: Futura Md and 2Peas A Beautiful Mess • **Paper:** KI and AL • **Rub-ons:** Doodlebug Designs • **Stamps:** Hero Arts and Rubber Moon

By Jennifer

I AM 38 TODAY

By Mellette

Cut chipboard into two photo corners; cover with craft glue. Arrange various beads on chipboard corners. Allow to dry completely. Cover beaded corners with Diamond Glaze and let dry.

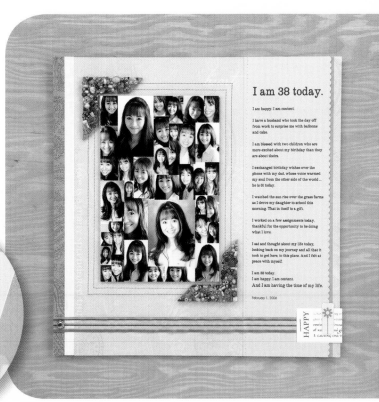

Beads: Westrim and Magic Scraps • **Flower:** KI • **Font:** Roundslab Serif • **Liquid sealer:** Diamond Glaze • **Paper:** AL and Anna Griffin • **Ribbon:** Michaels • **Sticker and brad:** MM

THEN SHE WAS 2 By Ashley

To create stamped embellishments, adhere several stamped images to chipboard. Embellish images with pen details, micro-beads, watercolors and glossy accents.

Buttons: AL • **Liquid adhesive:** Glossy Accents • **Matte gel:** Tri-Art • **Paint:** Pentel • **Paper:** Mustard Moon, AL and DMD • **Pen:** Zig • **Photo corners:** Ideal • **Sequins:** Doodlebug Designs • **Stamps:** Ma Vinci and Leave Memories

By Rhonda TWIRLABILITY

AFFIX PHOTOS to layout. Draw flowers on cardstock and use paper piercer to poke holes along the outline. Use crewel yarn to satin stitch flowers. Make French knots for the centers. Cut out and attach to layout. Cut journaling into strips. Use blanket stitch on random edges of layout.

Fonts: AL Worn Machine and Porcelain • **Rub-ons:** AL • **Yarn:** Nancy's Knit Knacks

TYING
THE KNOT

By Candice

Punch holes around a 12"x12" background (1" apart). Tie knots with wide satin ribbon through each hole. Adhere photo to background. Paint chipboard frame red, then coat with Glossy Accents. Adhere crystals to frame. Back frame with journaling printed in red. Print journaling in red and cut to size for frame.

Paper: SEI • **Ribbon:** Midori

ANATOMY OF A ROLL

Use a graphics program to design spirals in several sizes. Print on heavyweight paper. Paint with watercolors and cut out. Embellish with jewels and brads and mount some on black circles or on metal-rimmed tags.

By Lisa

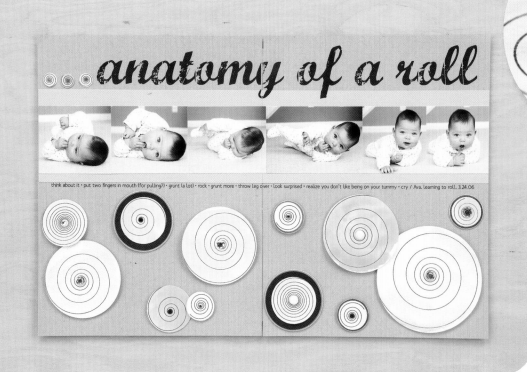

Brads: AC
Fonts: Marcelle Script and Serifa BT
Jewels and pearls: Westrim
Watercolors: Angora

By Danielle FLORIDA

CREATE A 12"x12" canvas in Photoshop. Layer the flower motif brushes, then print each stamped brush separately onto coordinating colors of cardstock. Cut out the flowers, then layer them onto layout. Embellish with brads, buttons and stitching.

Brads: Queen & Co. • **Buttons:** AL and Dill Buttons • **Chalk pencils:** General's • **Digital brushes:** Jason Gaylor • **Font:** AL Flighty • **Paper:** Daisy D's • **Rickrack:** Maya Road • **Rub-ons:** EK Success • **Tape:** Art Quest

HOMEBODIES
By Margie

PAINT A strip of foam core with decoupage medium. Cover the strip with small pieces of decorative paper. Apply decoupage medium over the top. Paint edges with acrylic paint and add brads. Cut a heart from foam core. Paint with decoupage medium and cover the heart with patterned paper.

Paper: My Mind's Eye, Bo Bunny and BG ● **Photo:** Tara Whitney ● **Stickers:** AC

TRUE TO YOU
By Mellette

Create design using digital brushes and print on a transparency. Cut transparency into three strips the same size as the microscope slides. Attach strips behind microscope slides. Glue pressed flowers to page. Attach microscope slides over pressed flowers to protect flowers and to serve as the stems.

Crystal brad: MM ● **Digital brushes:** Rhonna Swirls By Rhonna Farrer from www.twopeasinabucket.com ● **Flowers:** Pressed Petals ● **Fonts:** Weekdays Roman Slant and Avant Garde ● **Microscope slides:** VWR Scientific Inc. ● **Paper:** Anna Griffin and MM ● **Watch hand:** Walnut Hollow

Brad: Bazzill • Button: Dill Buttons • Lace and metal letters: AC • Paper: AL, Prima, Cherry Arte and BG • Pens: Zig and Uniball • Ribbon, stickers and rickrack: MM

Sketch an owl onto several patterned papers. Use different pieces of the owl from each patterned paper and piece together to create the owl. Outline the entire owl and the eyes with a black pen. Cut a tree from patterned papers and adhere to layout along with the owl.

By Danielle

BOUTIQUE TREASURES

CUPCAKES By Robyn

Draw a cupcake base and icing top onto paper. Trace the same shapes onto patterned paper and cardboard, then cut out. Create a mixture of blue paint and glitter glue and brush onto the cardboard. Stamp onto brown cardstock. Use the painted cardboard piece for the other cupcake base. Cut an icing top from white felt, brush with paint/glitter mixture and stamp onto another piece of cardstock. Add beads, French knots and small pompoms for the sprinkles.

Font: NotnorvalHmk and AL Uncle Charles ● **Paper:** MM ● **Rhinestone gems:** Hero Arts ● **Rub-ons:** AL

Chipboard flourish: Fancy Pants ● **Glitter glaze:** Li'l Davis ● **Heart gems:** Michaels ● **Rub-ons:** AL

LOVE By Candice

Adhere photos along the top and bottom of layout. Wrap tulle around the center of the page and tape to the back. Cut out hearts from pink and red cardstock. Use stitching rub-ons around the edges. Mount red hearts onto purple cardstock and cut out with scalloped scissors. Affix hearts across center of layout along with a large heart that contains the journaling cut into strips. Paint flourish red and top with a clear glitter glaze. Adhere flourish to the bottom of the journaling heart.

Don't you love it when you find a new, inventive use for an older product hidden in your massive scrapbook stash? Let our artists delight you by demonstrating fun ways to use ordinary items. Look at Renee's ingenious use of stickers to create an entire page of journaling on "Crazy Boy." And check out Gillian's paper clip embellishment on her "Attitude Swaggers" layout. You'll also see

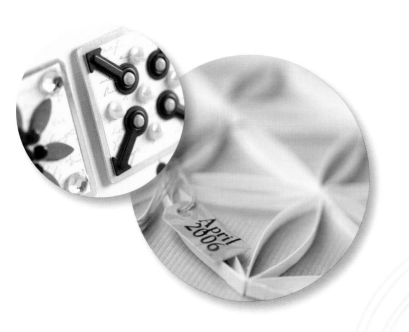

EVERYDAY DELIGHTS

how to utilize pre-made embellishments as a special detail on your project. You'll love seeing fresh uses for easily accessible products that will add exquisite details to your layouts.

LOVE TAGS

By Jackie

Flashcards: EK Success
Ribbon: SW and May Arts
Stickers: AC and EK Success

CREATE THREE tags with a folded edge on one end. Add alphabet flashcards and short greetings with letter stickers to each. Finish off with a ribbon tab or tie.

MERRY X-MAS
By Candice

CUT SCALLOP edges from scallop cardstock to fit across top and bottom of 8 ½"x11" page. Adhere patterned paper to center of page. Cut out triangles with scallop scissors to create banner. Mount sticker letters to the triangles; add crystals under each letter. Glue the tops of the triangles to a ribbon to create banner. Place red circle stickers in the scallops at the bottom of the layout. Spell "XMAS" with sticker letters; adhere crystals under each circle. Add more scallops to middle of the layout along with photo and journaling.

Photo corners: Advantus •
Ribbon: Midori
• **Stamp:** MM
• **Stickers:** CI

THOSE EYES
By Mellette

APPLY DECORATIVE rub-ons to plastic watch covers. Mix and layer rub-ons of various designs and colors. Adhere watch covers on layout.

Paper: Scenic Route, AL and BG • **Ribbon, buckle, gem sticker and crystal brad:** MM •
Rub-ons: BG, AL, Scrapworks, MM and KI • **Tab:** KI • **Watch covers:** Deluxe Plastic Arts and KI

ATTITUDE SWAGGERS

By Gillian

CREATE A design element using shaped paper clips. Adhere clips to background by dipping several sections of the clip in Diamond Glaze and quickly place in the desired position on the page.

Floral-shaped clips: Pier 1 Imports • **Label:** 7gypsies • **Shaped clips and studs:** Scrapworks • **Stickers:** AC • **Tags:** CI

HELLO VALENTINE

By Ashley

Gesso: Tri-Art • **Label and ribbon:** MM • **Paper:** Scenic Route, Chatterbox, Scrapworks, DMD and MM • **Sequins:** Doodlebug Designs • **Stamps:** MM and Ma Vinci's Reliquary

Piece together papers on background. Outline a heart shape with wire. Wrap the bottom of heart with wire as well. Add curls at ends of wire. Back wire heart accents with patterned paper. Add to layout along with vellum butterflies. Hand cut title from brown cardstock and swipe messy white paint around edges. Paint acetate hearts with gesso and stamp letters onto hearts.

FLOWERS
By Jennifer

USE INDEX prints or other small photos in brads or charms for the center of flowers.

Font: Kartika • **Paper:** K&Co., 7gypsies, Anna Griffin, MAMBI, AL and SW • **Photo corners:** Advantus

PLAY
By Margie

Cover a large portion of layout in words using letter stickers. Place pop dots under title letter stickers. Add hand sewn stitches to add detail to the title.

Paper: Kaleidoscope and BG • **Ribbon:** BG • **Stickers:** MM and Doodlebug Designs • **Stitches:** MM

BOLD OR BORING

By Leslie

PRINT DINGBAT snowflakes in various sizes onto inkjet transparency. Paint the backside of transparency and allow to dry. Affix to layout with pop dots and embellish with gems.

Charm accessories: 7gypsies • **Font:** Futura BdCn BT and WWSnowflake • **Gems:** Westrim • **Number charm:** K&Co. • **Paper:** BG, KI and AL • **Ribbon:** Stemma

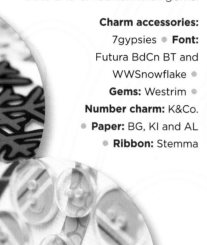

PRINT TITLE and text; adhere photos. Cut and punch circles from patterned papers. Adhere to page and cover with clear buttons arranged in patterns.

Buttons: AL • **Fonts:** Serifa BT and Serifa Thin BT • **Paper:** Chatterbox and KI

By Lisa ELLA'S FAVORITE THINGS

YOUTH GROUP RETREAT

By Mellette

Create three strips each consisting of patterned paper, cardstock and a photo, mixing the order on each strip. On each one, attach two paperclips to the top and two paperclips to the bottom. Turn strips over and tape paperclips to the back. Attach strips to the background. Thread ribbon through paperclips and tie so the ribbons connect each pair of paperclips vertically.

laugh enjoy
GOOD TIMES

Sacred Heart Catholic Church
Youth Group Retreat
May 12 - 14, 2006
Camp Cho-Yeh, Livingston, Texas

The high school youth group from our church had such a great time on their retreat this spring. Activities included rock climbing, swimming, singing, going on a trust walk, playing group games, and more. They also had discussions about faith, God, and inner strength. It was a very fun, inspiring, & motivating experience and I am so happy that Maysie had the opportunity to take part in it.

Maysie - 15, freshman yr

Font: Placard Condensed • **Paper:** AL, Cross My Heart, KI and Chatterbox • **Paperclips:** EK Success • **Ribbon:** MM, AL, May Arts, KI and Michaels • **Stickers, chipboard, flowers and brads:** MM

A BRIGHT AND SHINING MOMENT

By Gillian

PRINT STAR pattern on cardstock with light colored ink. Working in small sections, apply clear glue over design, using a small paintbrush to spread it evenly. Shake glitter over wet glue and let sit for a moment. Tap extra glitter off into a small tray and re-use for the next area.

Brads: Scrapworks • **Glitter:** Joann's Essentials • **Stickers:** Doodlebug Designs, AC and Chatterbox

this weekend, something clicked. you finally figured out how to ride your bike sans training wheels. you said, "I think I get it now!", pushed off, and that was all there was to it. a bright and shining moment. for you, definitely, but also for us. it makes our own hearts swell with pride to see you so proud of yourself. rock on, ky.

UTTER CLUTTER

By Marilyn

Collect scraps from previous projects. Paint larger papers with watercolors. Tear and adhere to top and bottom of page. Stamp old receipt with bubble wrap and paint. Add smaller bits of papers and items along top and bottom of page. Circle each with a colored pencil. Add photo; journal around them and fill in any empty spaces with a colored pencil.

Paper: AL • **Watercolors:** Angora

OUT ON A LIMB

By Robyn

O n scrap paper, draw a tree that you want to use as the stapled image. On the piece of cardstock you are using, staple the shape of the tree following the general drawing on the other piece of paper. On both sides of three staples, poke a small hole. Tie a knot in the ribbon to create the fruit and pull the ribbon through the holes on the sides of the ribbon to the back side of the page. For the border, staple a row of staples across the page. Loop ribbon underneath the staples.

Ribbon: MM and All My Memories
Die cut: Quickutz
Paper: KI and MM
Rub-on: Chatterbox

M&C **By Kelli**

T ear vellum into strips from a variety of green and blue shades. Using a glue stick, adhere the vellum to the page. Overlapping the pieces will create additional variations of the colors. Fill in empty spots with origami mesh and green floral tape. Splatter watercolor paints around the edges for a sea spray effect.

Buttons: AL •
Sequins: Westrim

FAITH IN ALL FORMS

By Danielle

CUT BOTTOMS off metal-rimmed hearts. Arrange around photo and stitch to patterned paper with embroidery floss. Copy Tibetan image and print on patterned paper. Stamp title.

Die cuts: Paper Adventures. • **Greeting card:** Chronicle Books • **Paper:** AL, BG and KI • **Pen:** Zig and Uniball • **Rhinestone and sequins:** Westrim • **Ribbon:** Michaels • **Rub-ons:** AL and 7gypsies • **Stamps:** Technique Tuesday and Fontwerks

COMPASSION

By Jennifer

Adhere sequins in a pattern. Stitch in place. Stitch a large circle around journaling to draw in the eye.

Font: Winterthur Condensed • **Paper:** Paper Fever • **Rub-ons:** MM • **Sequins:** Hero Arts and Doodlebug Designs

Adhere photos to background. Affix a strip of teal twill to the left side of layout. Add various sizes and shapes of tags. Use each tag as a mini canvas in order to create a collage.

By Leslie

MOM'S ADVICE

BE bold
love yourself

mom's advice

OTHERS

Smile and the world smiles with you!

don't forget

K L 4

shine

Be silly

Love is patient and kind

Buttons: AL and Doodlebug Designs • **Flower:** Fancy Pants • **Flower brads and tags:** MM • **Paper clip:** Stemma • **Paper:** SEI and AL • **Photo corner:** Advantus • **Rhinestones and tags:** Westrim • **Rub-ons:** BG • **Sticker and acrylic word:** KI • **Transparency and metal-rimmed tags:** CI • **Twill:** AL

BE bold
love yourself
mom's advice

By Ashley CHRISTMAS 57

PIECE TOGETHER Christmas tree from patterned paper and cardstock; set with a variety of eyelets. Cut swirls from vellum and add to tree; set with lots of small white eyelets. Remove paper from metal-rimmed tags, back with patterned paper and add blue eyelets. Top tree with vintage postage stamp set inside large metal concho/eyelet.

Eyelets: AC, MM, Scrappin' Extras, Doodlebug Designs and SW • **Paper:** Mustard Moon, Chatterbox, MM, Anna Griffin, AC and BG • **Pen:** Sakura • **Photo corners:** Advantus • **Stamps:** Fontwerks and Ma Vinci • **Tags:** Avery and AL

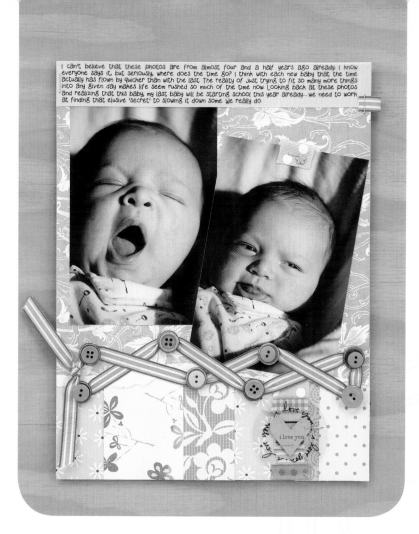

I can't believe that these photos are from almost four and a half years ago already. I know everyone says it, but seriously, where does the time go? I think with each new baby that the time actually has flown by quicker than with the last. The reality of just trying to fit so many more things into any given day makes life seem rushed so much of the time now. Looking back at these photos and realizing that this baby, my last baby will be starting school this year already... we need to work at finding that elusive 'secret' to slowing it down some. We really do.

Brads: Karen Foster ● **Chipboard heart:** Advantus ● **Font:** 2Peas Milkshake ● **Paper:** AL, Scenic Route, Paper Salon and Crate Paper ● **Ribbon:** Strano, May Arts and Michaels ● **Stamp:** Savvy Stamp

SLOW DOWN
By Jackie

To make brad accents, start with large size brads and adhere buttons on top. Attach brads to layout where desired, leaving them just loose enough to lace ribbon around; tie ribbon and then tighten up the brads.

IS HE JEALOUS OF HER? By Lisa

ADHERE SQUARE of patterned paper to white background. Using a graphics program, format title and text strip along with lines ending with black circles; print. Fill centers of square metal-rimmed tags with white paper stamped with a script image. Create a pattern on each one using photo turns, gems and brads. Add photos and large brads.

Brads: MM and AC ●
Fonts: VistaSansBook and VistaSansBlack ● **Gems and pearls:** Westrim ● **Paper:** Sassafrass Lass ● **Photo turns:** MM, 7gypsies and K&Co. ●
Stamp: Hero Arts

ROSY WINTERY CHEEKS

By Jackie

WRAP HEMP cording around the layout at various angles; tie off on the back. For the snowflakes, tie small lengths of the hemp at one point and string beads onto a few sections. Punch varying sizes of circles for snowflake ends and glue them to the layout; adhere the hemp ends onto the circles.

Beads and hemp: Westrim • **Font:** 2Peas Old Type • **Paper:** Scenic Route and My Mind's Eye • **Stickers:** Doodlebug Designs

PAINTED CARD SET

By Margie

Paint cardstock with various colors of acrylic paint. Cut out the paper and piece together designs using the strips and shapes. Add fine pen details to give shapes definition.

Chipboard: Advantus • **Paper:** My Mind's Eye and Paper Source • **Sticker:** Doodlebug Designs

YO-YO
By Ashley

Layer white vellum or mylar over script-printed vellum. Cut large paisley/swirl yo-yo design from dark blue cardstock; begin to layer additional swirls, scallops, circles, etc. around paisley and build shape. Secure vellum under cardstock or chipboard embellishments. Set some scallops and details with brads. Add handwritten title to white mylar swirl using permanent black ink and fill in color using watercolor pencils.

Chipboard: Bazzill ● **Paper:** Anna Griffin ● **Photo corners:** Advantus ● **Rhinestones:** Joann's ● **Watercolor pencil:** Lyra

A SIMPLE CONVERSATION
By Rhonda

Adhere photo at top of page. Use pre-cut quilling strips cut to 4 1/4". Fold at 2" mark, leaving a 1/4" overhang. Fold 1/4" piece over the end of the 2" piece and glue down. Pinch in fingers to create the roundness of the petal. Glue flower petals down in pattern shown. Hand cut scallops from patterned paper and attach. Adhere trim in wave pattern. Cut journaling into circle shape; cut off part of the circle along the left hand border.

Digital Brush: ChickPea digital kit from www.twopeasinabucket.com ● **Font:** American Typewriter ● **Paper:** SEI ● **Stamp:** MM ● **Tag:** K&Co. ● **Trim:** May Arts

By Jackie **KNEES & TOES**

Trace each chipboard piece onto patterned paper and cut out the shape. Cover the front of each chipboard piece with adhesive. Adhere patterned papers to chipboard and trim or sand off any extra edges.

Chipboard: Fancy Pants
Papers: MAMBI, AC and Paper Loft
Ribbon: May Arts

MADE FOR EACH OTHER

By Mellette

LAYER PATTERNED paper and photo on white background. With a pencil, lightly draw a heart shape over papers and photo. Machine stitch over pencil markings several times. (Each layer of stitching should not fall perfectly in line with the previous layer.) Randomly glue sewing notions over stitching. Tie ribbon around sewing gauge and attach to layout, securing end with mini brad.

Fonts: AL Script Hand and AL Post Master • **Paper:** Daisy D's and AL • **Pearl brad:** AL • **Ribbon:** Chatterbox

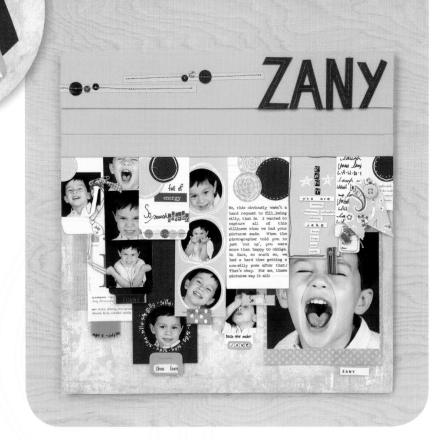

By Renee

ZANY

Incorporate numerous tabs into a project. Create tabs from plastic index file labels, pre-made cardstock tabs, ribbons and sequins, and use sticky note tabs, fabric labels and trimmed index cards. Attach photos and journaling to various pieces, adding to the layout by stitching them onto background in various levels.

Font: Crud • **Labels:** Advantus • **Metal letter:** MM • **Paper:** My Mind's Eye and BG • **Pen:** Sharpie • **Ribbon:** Offray • **Safety pin:** Hero Arts • **Tabs:** KI and AL • **Twill and buttons:** AL • **Waxed linen:** Paper Moon

BABY JOURNAL **By Leslie**

COVER THE front of a chipboard journal with a tape runner or other adhesive. Cut a variety of twill and adhere directly onto the cover, leaving space for a row of photos. Embellish the front with an initial layered on a button and a vintage metal flower. Hang a charm from twill on the binding.

Beads: Blue Moon Beads • **Charms:** MM • **Corsage pin:** Westrim • **Journal, twill and hardware:** 7gypsies • **Quotes and twill:** AL

it's a girl...a little beauty, an angel, and I'm madly in love with her.

By Margie

Buttons: AL • **Letter stickers:** Doodlebug Designs • **Ribbon and twill:** AL, Strano and Offray

LITTLE PLOT OF EARTH

USE DECORATIVE triangles to give a party/celebratory feel to the layout. Cut triangles from cardstock; cover in decoupage. Add scraps of ribbon. When dry, adhere buttons with glue dots.

HAWAIIAN BORN

By Rhonda

ATTACH THREE photos across layout. Add chipboard borders above and below photos. Apply decorative tape on the bottom border, then sand some of it away. Loop embroidery floss around the top border and let it hang. Adhere patterned paper cut with decorative scissors across the top and bottom. Make title from chipboard letters and stickers. Layer silhouette flowers, silk petals and paper flowers to create a flower accent.

Chipboard strips, letters, tape and silhouette shapes: Advantus • **Flowers:** Prima • **Font:** American Typewriter • **Letter stickers:** Scrapworks • **Paper:** Carolee's Creations and My Mind's Eye

Use envelopes in various styles, sizes and colors to create an interesting backdrop for photos. Add decorative stitching on envelope flaps and apply rub-ons to a few of the envelopes. Cut a rectangular shape from one of the envelopes and frame with a label holder. Tuck journaling inside so it shows through the opening. Punch a circle through one envelope flap, adhere contrasting cardstock underneath and embellish with camera charm.

PHOTOGRAPHIE
By Mellette

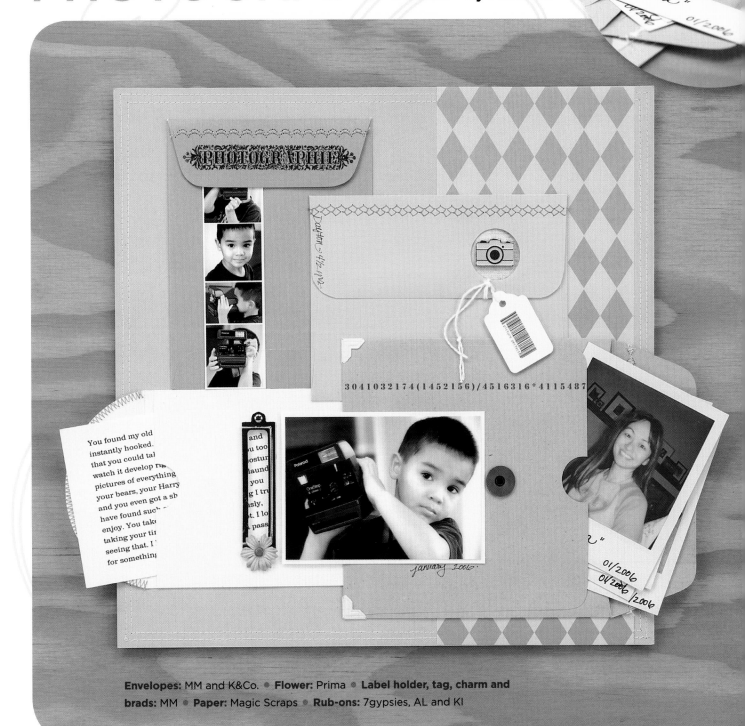

Envelopes: MM and K&Co. ● **Flower:** Prima ● **Label holder, tag, charm and brads:** MM ● **Paper:** Magic Scraps ● **Rub-ons:** 7gypsies, AL and KI

THE THUMP
By Lisa

USE A graphics program to format dotted lines and large black circles along each side border; print. Fill each circle with a printed transparency and an enamel accents. Arrange patterned paper, photos, text and punched black dots.

Enamel accents: MM ● **Fonts:** BlackJack and VistaSansAltReg ● **Paper:** BG and Kaleidoscope ● **Transparency:** CI

DREAMER
By Patricia

Cut one circle from orange and two circles from pink cardstock, approximately the size of the photos to be used; adhere to background paper. Cut a brown, curved design and adhere to layout. Draw white dots around inside edges. Adhere photos onto circles and then onto background. Print three sun shapes, cut into circles and affix a button to the center. Cut journaling into strips.

Buttons: AL ● **Embellishments:** K&Co. ● **Font:** AL Highlight ● **Paper:** The Paper Company ● **Pen:** AC

EASTER EGG TRADITION

By Jackie

Back metal clips with patterned paper and then use over a ribbon to make a ribbon slide.

Brads: American Tag • **Clips:** SW • **Fonts:** 2Peas Masterpiece and Beef Broccoli • **Flowers:** Prima • **Paper:** Sassafras Lass • **Ribbon:** May Arts

Easter Egg Tradition

Next only to a visit from the Easter Bunny himself, dying eggs is your favourite thing to do this holiday season. We made sure that there were lots to do this year and i love these plain ones that you all did. The colours were so perfect for Easter and spring...they are still hanging around here!

·photos·
Apr 15·06

HAPPY BIRTHDAY

By Renee

Stamp inkpads directly onto background cardstock by masking off areas with Post-it notes and pressing inkpad firmly down. Outline edges of each color with stitching. Add various photos and embellishments mounted on pop dots. Cut out additional title letters and journaling to mount on layout.

Font: Rockwell ● **Ink:** Clearsnap

SHE
By Gillian

USE RESIN embellishments to form a grid on layout. Adhere journaling or photos within each box. Round and ink edges of journaling blocks.

Chipboard: Imagination Project ● **Gem brad:** MM ● **Resin embellishments:** KI ● **Transparent letter:** Advantus

FOREVER FRIENDS

By Mellette

With a pencil, lightly mark swirl design on bottom right of page. Poke evenly spaced holes along the pencil markings. Hand stitch swirl using a back stitch and embroidery floss. Attach die-cut flowers over stitching. Use pop dots to attach some of the flowers.

Brads and page pebble: MM • **Die cut flowers:** Sassafras Lass • **Font:** Roundslab Serif • **Metal clip:** Provo Craft • **Paper:** Sassafras Lass and KI • **Photos:** Julie Kulak

By Renee

Attach fabric labels to a cardstock background. Sew a grid pattern over the top. Cut out heart shape, adhering to cardstock background. Add additional stitching around heart. Attach cardstock piece to another background along with pictures and patterned paper. Apply additional heart stickers and a chipboard letter title.

Fabric labels: MAMBI and Joann's • **Paper:** BG • **Stickers:** Pebbles, Inc. • **Tabs:** AL

GOALIE
By Kelli

CUT FOUR long, rectangular strips of paper approximately ¾". Adhere each of the four strips to the back of the star, angling them slightly to overlap into a "v" shape at the end.

Font: AL Superior
Paper: KI, Kaleidoscope and MM ● **Stars:** Kaleidoscope

Buttons: AL
Chipboard: MM
Letters: K&Co
Paper flowers and sequins: Doodlebug Designs
Paper: KI, Scenic Route, Scrapworks, Chatterbox and DMD
Pen: Zig
Rhinestones: Westrim
Ribbon: May Arts
Rickrack: Wright's

By Ashley

CAT OUTDOORS

Piece together background with cardstocks and patterned paper; stitch around edges. Use chipboard stickers to add details to page. Place ribbon slides tied with ribbon in center of flowers and add tags to wire to create a whimsical group of flowers. Split a frame into four pieces to use as oversized photo corners.

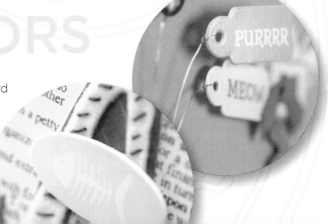

LOOKIN' GOOD

By Jennifer

CUT A LARGE star. Punch holes in epoxy stickers with hole punch. Add to layout and tie on tags.

Epoxy stickers: AL
Font: Futura MdCn BT

DOWN AND DERBY

By Marilyn

Cut a large circle from cardstock. Adhere to page. Stitch wide ribbon to page at an angle. Add additional ribbons to page. Assemble journaling strips, photos and cardstock rectangles to page. Apply sticker letters for title and sticker stars and cars to page.

Letter, star and car stickers: K&Co. **Rub-on:** AL

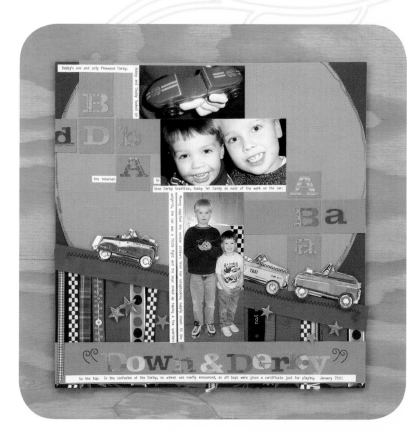

UNEXPECTED

Don't you envy the friend who easily converts a vintage window into a frame or striking home décor piece? You can feel the same euphoria with your scrapbooking stash. See how the creative Rhonda takes vintage linens and trims and transforms them into feminine details on her "Moments Like This" page. And look how cool circles cut from plastic placemats look on Jackie's "Good Morning" layout. This chapter is all about breaking down boundaries and adding dazzle to your projects with unexpected treasures. Find something that inspires you, then set forth to fashion details that strike your fancy.

TREASURES

COMFY ME

Letters: Advantus ● **Paper:** MM
● **Pens:** Sharpie, Galaxy Marker and Zig
● **Ribbon:** MM, AL and Doodlebug Designs

With my big teeth, loud laugh, long neck... in a bathing suit... finally comfy in my freckled skin

By Kelli

Cut rectangles from magazine ads in teal and aqua shades. Adhere to page in a sun burst design. Place the bamboo skewers on the page where desired. Poke a hole directly underneath the skewer.

Bring the ribbon through the hole from the back of the paper, loop it around the skewer and take the ribbon's end back through the same hole to the back of the paper. Tighten the ribbon on the back by taping it to the paper.

MOMENTS LIKE THIS

By Rhonda

ATTACH VINTAGE trims (lace, crochet, linen, ribbon) on cardstock. Add a strip of patterned paper and vintage buttons along the bottom piece. Use a vintage linen doily for photo mat. Attach photo, wings and button on top of flower. Print journaling on patterned paper and tuck partially under doily.

Font: 1942 Report • **Paper and angel wings:** AL

ALWAYS US

By Jennifer

Create textboxes in Word. Fill with color and change text to white. Punch into circles. Adhere wire-beaded bracelets for decoration.

Bracelets: Claire's • **Font:** WinterthurCondensed • **Frame:** Hobby Lobby • **Photo:** Tracie Radtke • **Tags:** MM

MAKING VALENTINES

By Marilyn

FLATTEN SMALL white cupcake liners and paint with watercolors. Let dry. Cut some liners into a continuous strip, forming spirals. Add half a sheet of circle-shaped paper to patterned paper sheet. Cover whole page with letter-printed vellum. Attach with brads. Adhere painted liners, photos, and liner strips to page. Sew a button to the center of some of the liners.

Buttons and rub-ons: AL • **Paper:** AL and AC • **Watercolors:** Angora

CREATE

By Gillian

Print the letter of choice on cardstock. Cut and glue pencil pieces over top of the printed letter, so the ink is no longer visible. Use as a large accent on a layout.

Font: Big Caslon • **Rub-ons:** AL • **Stickers:** Doodlebug Designs • **Transparencies:** CI

GOOD MORNINGS

By Jackie

ANGLE A calendar page on cardstock and add photos on top. Cut circle from a clear placemat and arrange over page elements.

Font: 2Peas Frazzled ● **Metal sun:** Carolee's Creations ●
Paper: AL ● **Ribbon:** Michaels ● **Stickers:** SW and SEI

By Cathy
WORRIED

Paint entire piece of cardstock with acrylic paint. While still wet, press a torn piece of tissue paper into paint, moving it around to give texture. When dry, apply another layer of paint and let dry. Sand around the edges. Paint one large and one small piece of spiral notebook paper. Add picture torn from an old book.

Charm: American Traditional ● **Font:** Courier New ● **Quote and sticker letters:** AL ● **Star stickers:** Target

COUNTRY LIVING

Use wood moldings and hardware washers for decorative elements on a layout. Make a butterfly from screen door mesh, hemp and paper. Add a duct tape border.

By Leslie

Font: Jailbird Jenna and Lucida Console • **Mesh:** MM • **Paper:** Chatterbox, BG and AL

love our country clothes-line

it is still a thrill finding deer grazing in the backyard

COUNTRY LIVING EST. 1999

woodsy backyard = room to roam

antiques filling our cozy home

we are lucky that our neighbours are our friends and family

it's a peaceful life, we love it

asks the questions / is highly curious / is mentally & physically involved / has wild, silly ideas / plays around, yet tests well / discusses in detail, elaborates / beyond the group / already knows / 1-2 repetitions for mastery / constructs abstractions / prefers adults / draws inferences / initiates projects / is INTENSE / creates a new design / [a gifted student · 4.2006]

ENJOYS LEARNING / good guesser / MANIPULATES INFORMATION / thrives on complexity / is keenly observant / is highly self-critical.

A GIFTED STUDENT

By Lisa

Adhere strips of patterned paper to background. Format text, title and black rectangle; print. Add photos. Drill holes in each end of ruler, thread with ribbon and adhere inside black box. Affix punched circles and staples.

Fonts: Serifa BT, FranklinGotDemCon, Interstate, Clarissa, VistaSansBlack, VistaSansBold, VistaSansAltLight, CHANL, Existence, Riverside, Trajan Pro, Rubberstamp, Highlight and Blackjack. •
Paper: BG and My Mind's Eye • **Ribbon:** Offray

GRANDPARENTS By Mellette

Remove plastic from centers of coin holders. Cover the fronts with patterned paper. Cut out paper from center of coin holder with a craft knife. Place photos and patterned paper behind some coin holders; leave the window open on the rest. Attach coin holders to page. Add embellishments to open centers, such as beads inside a watch cover, watch face with photo anchor, stickers, ribbon, etc.

Digital brushes: Black Eyed Pea, Chick Pea and Rhonna Swirls by Rhonna Farrer, downloaded from www.twopeasinabucket. com • **Flower:** K&Co. • **Font:** Chopin Script • **Mesh, rub-ons, photo anchor and brad:** MM • **Paper:** DCWV, KI, K&Co., 7gypsies and Carolee's Creations • **Ribbon:** Chatterbox • **Sticker:** AL • **Watch cover:** KI • **Watch face and tab:** 7gypsies

A NOTE TO MY GIRLS

A **note** to my girls
about being pregnant:

If your **pregnancies** are anything like
mine (let's hope not) there are some
things I don't want to forget to tell you –

Tums and **Sudafed** are your friends.
Eat a little, a lot.
Caffeine causes **restless** legs.
Buy a **good** bra.
Take your vitamin at night – especially at first.
Drinking **water** really does help.
Cheesy baked potatoes helped me
through the beginning.
When you feel a **headache** coming on,
nip it **immediately**.

I promise you it's worth it.
I promise.

Journaled while I was 7 months pregnant with your little brother.

Cut a whimsical tree trunk from cardstock. Using three shades of contact paper, cut various widths of strips and adhere on trunk both vertically and horizontally. Embellish with metal-rimmed tags.

By Cathy

Paper: KI

D IS FOR DADDY

By Kelli

COLLECT PLASTIC twist-tie holders from children's toys. Use on a layout as a frame. Secure with wire, brads and twist ties. Create a small book with pictures, drawings and photos. Affix to page with Velcro.

Brads: AC • **Paper:** DMD and MM • **Pen:** Zig • **Photo:** Tara Whitney

CHINATOWN

By Danielle

FOR THE scalloped edge of cocktail umbrellas, remove the paper from the umbrellas sticks, cut the circles in half and then layer behind photos.

Brads and buttons: AL • **Chipboard:** Advantus • **Cocktail umbrellas:** Cost Plus World Market • **Pen:** Zig • **Rhinestones:** Westrim • **Ribbon and rickrack:** MM and AL • **Stamps:** MM and Fontwerks

FEATHER COLLECTOR
By Patricia

Cut patterned paper to 11"x11"; adhere to center of blue cardstock. Lightly paint gray corrugated paper with white acrylic paint, let dry and adhere to center of layout. Print journaling onto mustard cardstock, cut out and ink edges. Add tie-tack brads to embellish. Adhere photos on top along with a chipboard and sticker letter. Attach feathers to layout and tie string through buttons.

Chipboard: Scenic Route ● **Corrugated paper:** Westrim ● **Font:** AL Constitution ● **Ink:** Tsukineko ● **Paper, tie tacks, tag and buttons:** AL ● **Pen:** AC ● **Stickers:** Doodlebug Designs

CHALLENGE By Jennifer

CUT ARCH in paper and tuck tags behind it; stitch in place.

Font: WinterthurCondensed ● **Letter stickers:** Doodlebug Designs ● **Paper:** Paper Fever

SO FORTUNATE

By Jamie

PAINT LOWER middle area of layout. Attach photos on either side. Attach fortunes in the middle and side. Hand write journaling and apply letter stickers. Print out bracket on transparency and attach to layout. Adhere a small strip of micro beads to bottom.

Bracket brush: www.twopeasinabucket.com • **Flowers:** Prima • **Letter stickers:** Li'l Davis • **Papers:** KI

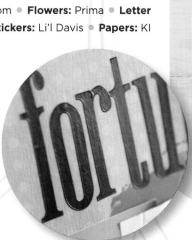

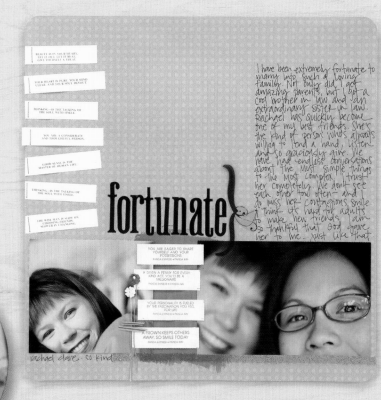

SUPER ROBOT MONKEY

By Jamie

Paint right hand side of layout. Print row of three photos and adhere to side of layout. Print journaling on transparency. Add main photo and toy packaging. Affix brads and stickers.

Brads and pen: AC • **Paper:** KI • **Stickers:** SW and 7gypsies

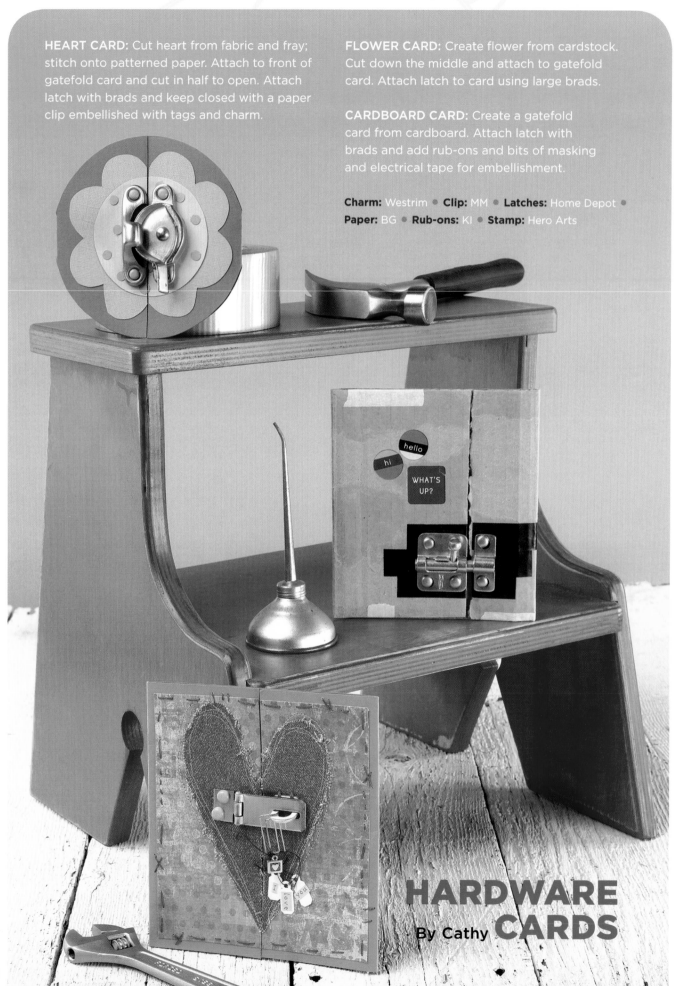

HEART CARD: Cut heart from fabric and fray; stitch onto patterned paper. Attach to front of gatefold card and cut in half to open. Attach latch with brads and keep closed with a paper clip embellished with tags and charm.

FLOWER CARD: Create flower from cardstock. Cut down the middle and attach to gatefold card. Attach latch to card using large brads.

CARDBOARD CARD: Create a gatefold card from cardboard. Attach latch with brads and add rub-ons and bits of masking and electrical tape for embellishment.

Charm: Westrim • **Clip:** MM • **Latches:** Home Depot • **Paper:** BG • **Rub-ons:** KI • **Stamp:** Hero Arts

hello
hi
WHAT'S UP?

HARDWARE CARDS
By Cathy

HAPPY
By Robyn

For the heart, fold and staple rubber bands into place. Tie rubber band into a knot and staple to page. Stamp a phrase onto rubber band. Combine many together to create a border; staple in place.

Font: AL Uncle Charles • **Ink:** StazOn • **Pen:** Stampin' Up! • **Stamps:** AL and Hero Arts

MAYSIE'S THOUGHTS
By Mellette

PAINT THE edges of the negative disks. Let dry. Apply decorative rub-on images onto the disks; attach disks to layout. Add sticker, flower or a ribbon brad to each disk's center opening.

Epoxy sticker: AL • **Flowers:** Prima • **Fonts:** Chopin Script from the Internet • **Paper:** DCWV and We R Memory Keepers • **Photo corner:** Canson • **Rub-ons:** AL and BG • **Tag and brads:** MM

Die-cut letters: Quickutz • **Fonts:** AL Uncle Charles and Courier New • **Paper:** KI • **Rub-ons:** AL

Cut the map into various pieces. Create three bowls of dye: red, purple and walnut ink (brown). Dip various sizes of the map into each dye and let dry overnight. Iron the map pieces so they are flat. Sew the pieces together like a quilt, with a 1/8" seam. Vary having the seam on the back and on the top.

SWITZERLAND By Robyn

MR. ROBOTO
By Kelli

PIECE TOGETHER puzzle pieces using scrapbook embellishments. Fill in any missing pieces with rub-ons or stickers. Journal using several types of rub-ons.

Puzzle: Children's stash

WHAT BECOMES
By Ashley

Paint torn piece of muslin with gesso and apply messy watercolors. Layer vellum and stamped notebook paper. Cut pieces of clear straws and arrange in heart shape; adhere to page with Glossy Accents. Place strips of journaling into pieces of straw. Stitch around heart; add buttons, tape, etc. Place crumpled paper under large watch crystal and add title to the top.

Button: AL ● **Gesso:** Tri-Art ● **Letters:** K&Co. ● **Paper:** DMD ● **Photo corners:** Advantus ● **Rub-ons and watch crystal:** Scrapworks ● **Stamps:** Purple Onion ● **Tape:** 3M and 7gypsies ● **Watercolor:** Dr. Ph Martin's and Pentel

MY I LOVE YOU
By Jackie

Back embroidery hoops with patterned papers or cardstock, or if papers are lighter, reinforce them with chipboard. Fill some rings with photos. Arrange rings and glue together with hot glue.

Font: Daisy Script ● **Paper:** AL, Daisy D's, KI and Paper Salon

WHAT'S COOKING?

By Candice

Cover the book with patterned paper; sand the edges. Paint a wooden spoon with pink acrylic paint and let dry. Paint over with pink glitter glaze, doing multiple coats if necessary. Decorate tag with retro image, sticker and bookplate. Tie tags and charms to the spoon. Cut to size and adhere lined paper and recipe. Glue down lace at the bottom of the cover to give apron appearance.

Album: 7gypsies • **Bookplate and brads:** Junkitz • **Glitter glaze:** Li'l Davis • **Paper:** Scenic Route and MM • **Ribbon:** Midori • **Stickers:** Crafty Secrets

Paint papier-mâché boxes with acrylic paint. When dry, sand some areas to remove a little paint. Stamp or stencil sanded areas with a lighter shade of paint. Attach unique knobs on top.

Knobs: Home Depot ●
Stamps: MM

BOXES By Cathy

5 STAGES OF GRIEF

Buttons: AL ● **Chipboard:** Advantus and MM ● **Font:** AL Highlight ● **Mask:** Advantus ● **Paper:** Scenic Route

By Patricia

REMOVE PICTURE from four large puzzle pieces to reveal chipboard centers. Cover with patterned paper. Fit pieces together, lay a mask on top and paint with black acrylic paint; remove mask. Apply decoupage medium on top. Adhere three of the pieces to left side of layout. Adhere fourth piece to left side of layout along with main photo and journaling.

GALLERY *of*

What would you do if challenged to use 10 buttons on a page? What about 30 or even 70? In the Gallery of Miscellany, you'll see how these artists detail their work with a few or a lot of one embellishment. The row of small buttons on Jamie's "Els" page is a dainty touch to a baby layout, but a slew of buttons on Kelli's "Jump" plays up the fun, summery feel of the photo. Sometimes a few touches is enough detail and sometimes lots of touches—if artfully arranged—is what it takes to give a page punch! Stretch your creative imagination to create details that command attention.

MISCELLANY

ELS
By Jamie

Mat photo on handmade paper, then mat onto a larger piece of kraft cardstock. Trim strips of patterned papers and hand write journaling on one. Cut circles from patterned paper and adhere along with buttons under journaling. Using a paperclip, attach the title, a transparency strip and more ribbon.

Fabric tab: Scrapworks • **Ink:** Tsukineko • **Paper:** Artistic Scrapper, KI and AC • **Ribbon:** AC • **Rub-ons and buttons:** AL • **Stamp:** Hero Arts • **Stickers:** Doodlebug Designs • **Transparency and epoxy:** AL

OVERRATED
By Kelli

CUT A swoosh shape from chipboard. Ink the edges and adhere to page. "Mat" buttons on circles of wrapping paper. Stitch in place.

Buttons: AL • **Paper:** MM • **Pens:** Galaxy Marker and Zig

HANNAH

By Mellette

With a pencil and ruler, lightly mark evenly spaced diagonal lines for stitching. Machine stitch over markings. Arrange buttons over cross marks of diagonal stitching lines. Secure buttons with thread.

Hannah cute as a button

Hannah is the little girl who lives next door. She is so spunky and talkative. She loves to play in the treehouse with Dayton. And she is always barefoot. She likes to come over and play with our cats, and she always has something interesting to tell us. She is such a sweet little girl. We truly enjoy having her live next door. She brings so much energy and enthusiasm wherever she goes. *4.2006*

precious

Font: Commercial Script • **Metal signage:** MM • **Paper and buttons:** AL • **Ribbon:** May Arts and MM

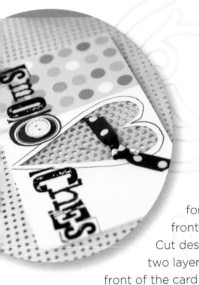

MAGIC MESH CARDS

By Gillian

USE MESH tape to form a window in the front of a greeting card. Cut desired shape through two layers of cardstock (the front of the card and one additional piece). Sandwich mesh tape between the two layers and adhere the layers together. Decorate the front of the card.

Acrylic letters: KI ● **Mesh tape:** Magic Mesh ● **Paper:** Doodlebug Designs, SW and Downtown Designs ● **Pen:** Marvy Uchida ● **Ribbon:** Offray ● **Rub-ons:** MM and AL ● **Stickers:** Doodlebug Designs and AC

WILL YOU? By Lisa

Use a graphics program to create a 12"x12" black-filled canvas. Add title and subtitle (at bottom), setting text to white; print. Create another 8"x12" pink-filled canvas. Add journaling strips, setting the text color to white. Print, trim and adhere to background. Add strips of printed gaffer tape, photos and embellishments.

Brads: AC ● **Flower:** MM ● **Fonts:** VistaSansBook, Marcelle Script, Bernard MT Condensed, Serifa BT, Rubberstamp and Clarissa ● **Gaffer tape:** 7gypsies

By Cathy

PEACE

Affix duct tape to background; add photo on top. Place black electrical tape to the left of photo and put journaling on top. Accent with pieces of masking tape here and there. Cover heart with masking tape and secure to page. Frame title with label holder.

Charm: Westrim • **Font:** 2Peas Weathervane • **Letter stickers:** MM • **Paper and label holder:** BG

UM-UM-UM-UM

By Cathy

TEAR OR cut several papers and decorative tape. Adhere to layout horizontally and vertically. Add journaling block and embellish with rub-ons and stitching.

Fonts: Euphorigenic, Stone Sans ITC and 2Peas Weathered Fence • **Rub-ons:** AL • **Tape:** Advantus

COUSINS
By Lisa

USE A graphics program to create an 8 ½"x11" orange-filled canvas. Add journaling with text set to white or paper; print. For left page, arrange text, lines and dots, then print. Fill metal-rimmed tags with punched papers and adhere in an arrow pattern.

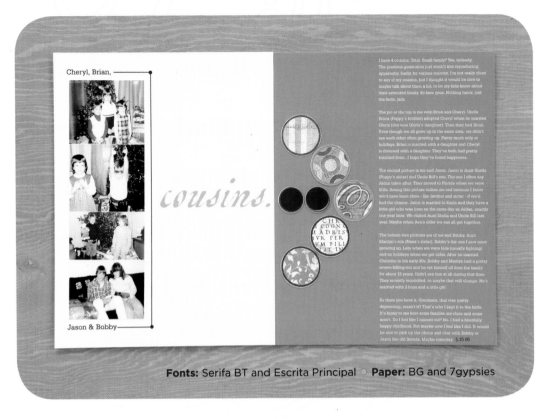

Cheryl, Brian,

cousins.

Jason & Bobby

Fonts: Serifa BT and Escrita Principal • **Paper:** BG and 7gypsies

the boy had a taste for the good life

ONE OF THE MOST MAGICAL THINGS ABOUT WATCHING A CHILD AT PLAY...THEY REALLY DO MARVEL AT, AND APPRECIATE THE SIMPLE THINGS IN LIFE MOST OF ALL. SNOW FALLING FROM THE SKY BECOMES A TASTY TREAT!

TASTE FOR THE GOOD LIFE
By Leslie

Use metal-rimmed circle tags as a backdrop for accents. Punch 1" circles to fill circle tags. Add acrylic snowflakes to the centers. For the scalloped border, cut the circle tags in half and add orange brads to some.

Brads: Carolee's Creations • **Font:** Fabianestem • **Paper:** KI and AL • **Puffy circles, photo corner and snowflakes:** Advantus • **Ribbon:** AC • **Tags:** Avery

By Mellette

WRAPPED

Using a tag-maker template, trace and cut out desired circles from white cardstock. Cover each circle with double-sided tape. Adhere ribbon to circles. Trim off excess ribbon. Use tag maker to make metal-rimmed tag. Attach to layout, using foam tape on a few to add dimension.

Brad and button: AL ● **Paper:** Scenic Route, KI, Scrappy Cat Creations and Paper Fever ●
Photo corner: Advantus ● **Photo turn:** 7gypsies ● **Ribbon:** KI, MM, Michaels and May Arts ●
Rub-ons and border sticker: KI ● **Stickers:** AC ● **Tag maker, metal rims and template:** MM

AMERICAN GIRL PLACE

By Margie

To create little handmade dolls, cut shapes (squares, triangles, circles) from various papers and assemble dolls. Accent with buttons and brads. Cover metal-rimmed tags with fabric or paper and attach dolls to the tags.

Button: AL ● **Paper:** Cloud 9 Designs, Scenic Route, BG and KI ● **Ribbon:** Offray ● **Tags:** MM

HE
By Rhonda

COVER CHIPBOARD accents with patterned paper. Rough up the edges with a craft knife. Adhere three different ribbon pieces to top right corner of layout, using a sticker to secure. Add title letters and journaling strips. Sand the edges of the layout to distress.

Chipboard shapes: Fancy Pants ● **Font:** AL Worn Machine ● **Ghost letters:** Advantus ● **Paper:** SEI ● **Ribbon:** Li'l Davis, Michaels and KI ● **Sticker:** 7gypsies

HAPPINESS
By Candice

Fold ribbon to create pleats and staple ribbon after each fold. Do this with four ribbons and then glue them down to the center of a 12"x12" background. Tape the end of the ribbon behind the background on the right side. Hand stitch around a matted photo. Add rub-ons and sparkly accents to photo. Fold large flower in half and adhere to the photo. Journal on a small strip of cardstock and adhere under the folded ribbon under the photo.

Flower: Advantus ● **Glitter:** Art Institute ● **Paper:** Kaleidoscope ● **Ribbon:** Midori, KI and Li'l Davis ● **Rub-ons:** Gin-X ● **Sticker:** MAMBI

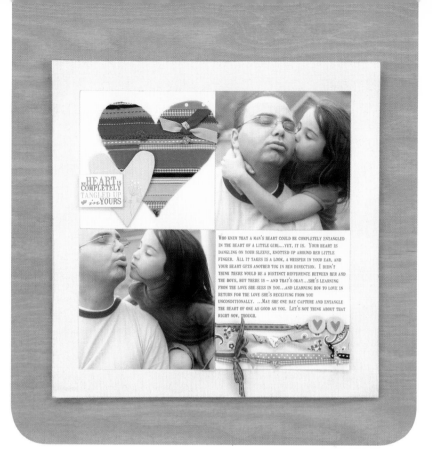

MY HEART **By Renee**

Attach various ribbons to a sticky adhesive surface, then cut into a heart shape. Add to page along with trimmed photos and journaling. Accent with additional ribbons tied together.

Who knew that a man's heart could be completely entangled in the heart of a little girl...yet, it is. Your heart is dangling on your sleeve, knotted up around her little finger. All it takes is a look, a whisper in your ear, and your heart gets another tug in her direction. I didn't think there would be a distinct difference between her and the boys, but there is — and that's okay...she's learning from the love she sees in you...and learning how to love in return for the love she's receiving from you unconditionally. ...May she one day capture and entangle the heart of one as good as you. Let's not think about that right now, though.

Chipboard: Heidi Grace ● **Font:** Mailart Rubberstamp ● **Ribbons:** Offray and AL

TIME
By Jennifer

CREATE TEXT and flip to print backwards on iron-on transfer paper. Iron onto ribbon.

Die-cut letters: Quickutz ● **Font:** Desert Dog, Hallmark ● **Photo:** Essenza Studio ● **Ribbon:** Offray, AC and KI ● **Sequins:** Queen & Co.

It is your time.
The time for you to turn your dreams into your reality.
The time for you to shine.
An exciting time of life
So many opportunities.
So many open doors.
Your optimism will take you far.
Nothing can stop you.
Enjoy this time.
You deserve the best.

"The future belongs to those who believe in the beauty of their dreams." - Your favorite quote by Eleanor Roosevelt.

Lauren Alyse
age 17

time

FABRIC CARDS

By Cathy

Fonts: Kirby and Broken Wing • **Paper:** BG and My Mind's Eye • **Stamp:** Hero Arts

Cut pieces from fabric, fray edges and adhere to cards. Machine stitch to accent.

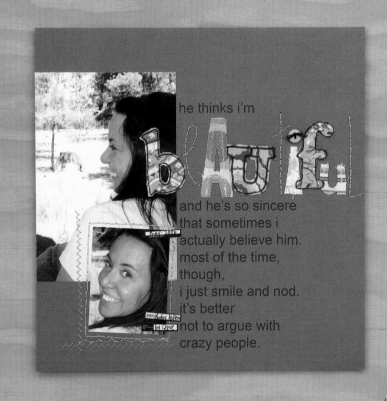

Button: SEI • **Labels:** 7gypsies • **Rub-on stitches:** K&Co. • **Stickers:** AC, Chatterbox and MM

HE THINKS I'M BEAUTIFUL

By Gillian

Create a title using hand-cut fabric letters. Lay letter sticker on top of fabric and trace around the sticker. Remove sticker and cut out letter. (Stickers can be re-used at a later time.) Staple or machine stitch letters to layout.

he thinks i'm b A U if L and he's so sincere that sometimes i actually believe him. most of the time, though, i just smile and nod. it's better not to argue with crazy people.

Brads: AL and MM • **Paper:** AL • **Tab:** 7gypsies

THRU THE YEARS By Leslie

Cut vintage fabric and patterned paper into 2" squares and adhere on brown cardstock background. Sew around each square and add a button or brad. Adhere heritage photos above each row of squares. Run journaling and fabric piping horizontally at top. Place title in an index tab; surround with fabric and buttons to finish.

IRON BACK of fabric to waxy side of freezer paper on low iron setting. Cut shapes from freezer paper-backed fabric. Collage onto layout with matte gel. Stitch along some edges of fabric to add definition. Apply white decorative rub-on to mylar, then frame with a painted metal ring. Affix letter stickers on pop dots and tie ring with vintage ribbon.

Label: MM • **Matte gel:** Tri-Art • **Pen:** Zig • **Rub-ons:** BG • **Stamps:** Magnetic Poetry • **Stickers:** AL • **Tag:** 7gypsies

DAYS IN THE SUN
By Ashley

PLAYGROUND

By Jennifer

CUT PATTERNED paper into waves; stitch to bottom of layout. Hand stitch a few beads along some lines.

Buttons: Buttons Galore
Font: Steepidien
Paper: KI, K&Co. and AL
Photo: Tina Parker

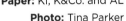

BE YOU

By Jackie

Make bead flourishes by stringing glass and alpha-beads onto wire, using glass beads as spacers between words. Wave the wires and twist ends into tight circles so beads will not fall off.

Beads and wire: Westrim • **Papers:** Mara Mi, Anna Griffin, BoBunny Press, AL, Daisy D's, K&Co, My Mind's Eye and 7gypsies • **Ribbon:** Michaels

By Danielle

MISSION DISTRICT

Paint small wooden beads and adhere for the lady's necklace. Hand stitch part of title. Adhere plastic pearl beads along center strip of paper.

Die cut: AL • **Paper:** AL and Urban Lily • **Pearl beads:** Cousin Corporation • **Pen:** Zig • **Stickers:** MM • **Wood beads:** Westrim

LAZY DAYS OF SUMMER

By Mellette

Trace several sizes of circles onto cardstock. Using a paper piercer, poke holes along pencil lines. Thread a beading needle with quilting or craft thread. Backstitch through the holes, adding beads before bringing the needle from front to back. After beading is complete, add journaling, title embellishment and accents inside circles.

Beads: Westrim and Magic Scraps • **Button:** Blumenthal Lansing Co. • **Metal signage, flower charm and ribbon brad:** MM • **Paper:** AL • **Ribbon:** Michaels

A GOOD MOTHER

By Mellette

CUT 12 diamond shapes from chipboard. Cover nine with glitter using super-tacky tape. For the remaining diamond shapes, adhere patterned paper and trim off excess paper. Use as a page border.

Button: 7gypsies • **Digital brushes:** Rhonna Swirls by Rhonna Farrer from www.twopeasinabucket.com
Fonts: Sylfaen and Porcelain • **Glitter:** Sulyn Industries • **Gloss sealer:** Diamond Glaze • **Paper:** DCWV, KI and
Anna Griffin • **Photo corner:** Advantus • **Ribbon:** KI • **Sequin flowers:** Westrim • **Super tape:** Therm O Web

GOLD By Patricia

CUT OUT a curved border design, then cover with glue and glitter. Let dry. Print journaling onto green cardstock. Adhere glitter border to green cardstock and cut along outside edge. Adhere to patterned paper. Affix butterfly. Mat focal photo, then adhere all photos. Hand cut title, add glitter and adhere to layout.

Font: AL Cadence • **Glitter:** Stampendous • **Paper:** Carolee's Creations

This year in preschool, Madisyn has been working on writing the letters in the alphabet. However, the only one that she can write, is the letter 'M'. "My name starts with the letter, Mmmmmmm!" she says. And every time she sees a word that has the letter 'M', she says it again and again. Now we just need to teach her how to write the other 25 letters of the alphabet! Madisyn - July 2006

THE LETTER "M"

By Robyn

Using pre-made glitter stickers, alternate the angle of the stickers on a piece of cardstock. To create the strips of glitter, use a tacky tape. Apply to layout, take off the protective covering and shake glitter on the tape. Be sure to spray with a fixative to keep the glitter from falling off.

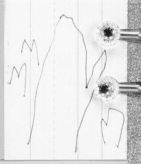

Chipboard letter: Advantus
File card: Lovely Design **Font:** AL Uncle Charles **Glitter alphabet stickers, tag and flowers:** MM **Paper:** KI, MM and Chatterbox
Pen: Stampin' Up!
Photo turns: 7gypsies

Brads: AC • **Fonts:** Lucida Bright, Pigiarniq and 2Peas You Are Here • **Paper:** BG • **Stamps:** Hero Arts, Simply Stamped and Penny Black

IF I WAS PRESIDENT
By Lisa

Stamp images on tags with watermark ink. Heat emboss with clear embossing powder. Paint with watercolors and the stamped images will resist the paint. Arrange in a border pattern and attach with brads. Create title in a graphics or photo-editing program, altering each letter size, alignment, fill and stroke.

FUN ALL DAY LONG
By Leslie

LAYER A printed transparency over green patterned paper, then add purple cardstock behind the transparency to fill in the circle area. Cut 2"x3" photos into a tag shape and attach to layout with brads. Embellish layout with photo corners, circle tags, buttons and acrylic accents.

Acrylic accents: KI • **Buttons:** AL • **Chipboard floral accent:** CI • **Flower stickers:** K&Co. • **Fonts:** After Hours and Impact • **Paper:** AL Rhonna Farrer • **Photo corners:** Chatterbox • **Quote:** My Mind's Eye • **Transparency:** Hambly

STARE
By Jamie

Cut a circle from patterned paper. Back it with a solid piece of cardstock. Adhere photos. Add a swirl clip tied with ribbon. Affix tags; staple transparent letters over the top and journal underneath.

Clip: Scrapworks • **Font:** 2Peas Bamboo • **Paper and letters:** KI • **Ribbon:** AC

SECRETS
By Marilyn

Paint and stamp tags of all sizes. Keep the strings on some. When dry, assemble on page. Print title and place under a painted chipboard bookplate. Print journaling on larger photo. Trim smaller photo to size and paint edges.

Chipboard bookplate: BG • **Font:** 2Peas Austin • **Stamps:** PSX, Hero Arts and Uptown Design Company • **Watercolors:** Angora

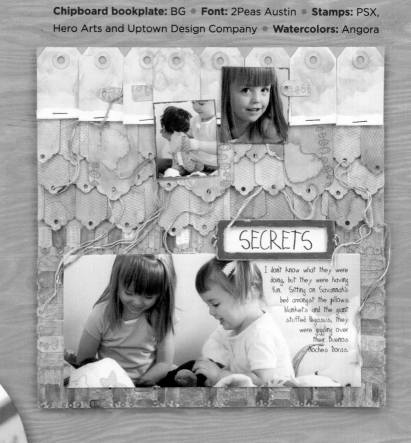

BECOME

By Jamie

Arrange patterned papers down left side. Adhere ribbon along left side of arrangement. Paint bottom section of layout and hand journal. Add paisley chipboard and place gems on the dots. Tie ribbon to chipboard and dangle tag with jump ring. Add jewels to the top paper. Embellish a wooden frame with words and gems.

Chipboard: We R Memory Keepers • **Frame:** Chatterbox • **Gems and stamp:** Hero Arts • **Paper:** KI and AC • **Rub-ons and stickers:** 7gypsies • **Tag and jump ring:** MM

SISTERS **By Cathy**

Adhere photo in center of layout and stitch around the edges. Create clusters of white embellishments around border of page. Embellish with crystal gems. Pink one edge of journaling and stitch to page.

Flowers: Advantus • **Gems:** Westrim • **Paper:** My Mind's Eye • **Ribbon:** MM and Offray • **Stamp:** MM

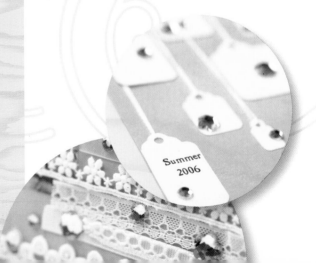

BURST
By Danielle

Adhere gems to chipboard diamonds, then adhere to layout. Punch different-sized holes from the bottom left corner and back with white cardstock. Make background from lots of rub-ons. Hand letter title.

Chipboard: Advantus • **Paper:** Prima • **Pen:** Zig and Uniball • **Reinforcers and stickers:** 7gypsies • **Rhinestones:** Westrim • **Rub-ons:** BG, 7gypsies, AL and MM

2 BY 2 By Mellette

BACK LABEL holders with cardstock. Glue gems to cardstock inside label opening. Attach label holders to page, tying some with string and securing with crystal brads. Tie ribbon to end of label holder at the edge of the page. Glue gems to journaling strip and subtitle.

Chipboard circles and flower: KI • **Font:** Roundslab Serif • **Gems:** Westrim • **Label holders, brads, stickers and rub-ons:** MM • **Paper:** AL • **Ribbon:** AC and Michaels

TAG SET By Cathy

SNOWFLAKE TAG: Cover a tag with 1" squares cut from blue paper. Embellish with a variety snowflake sequins. Attach quote and hang tag with thin wire.

HEART TAG: Adhere two hearts onto tag. Sand and cut the edges of the tag with pinking sheers. Stitch around the hearts, adding sequins in the stitching. Add twill and greeting.

BIRD TAG: Stamp bird onto yellow patterned paper and cut out just the beak. Stamp bird onto purple paper and cut out just the body. Assemble bird and mat on white cardstock, cutting around the image. Adhere three rows of sequins and a strip of green paper to tag; affix bird on top. Add greeting and twine tie.

Font: French Script and Slurry • **Paper:** BG, My Mind's Eye and AL • **Sequins:** Doodlebug Designs, Tinsel Trading, Westrim and Bath and Body Works • **Stamp and twill:** AL

HOLY COMMUNION By Jackie

Trim and position photos on cardstock background. Add paper blocks and journaling; cover all seams with ribbon and trim. Randomly adhere sequins to one block. Finish with silk flowers.

Paper: Anna Griffin, AL, Scenic Route and Daisy D's • **Ribbon:** Flair, MM and May Arts • **Sequins:** Westrim and Queen & Co.

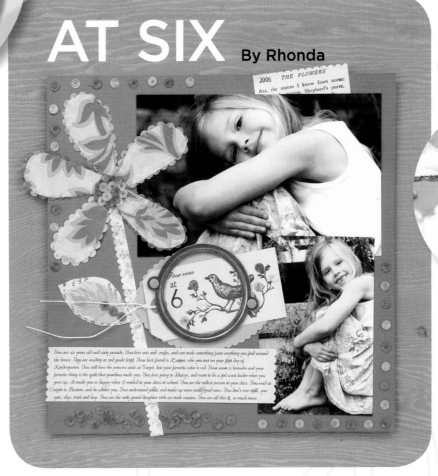

AT SIX By Rhonda

Cut flower petals from fabric. Adhere sequins around the edges of the backside of the petals. Cut center of flower from cardstock and cover with sequins. Cut leaf from book paper and layer fabric and sequins on top. Adhere photos on page along with pieced flower. Layer scalloped card and bird tag under large bookplate. Accent the rest of layout with more sequins.

Bookplate: BG ● **Border sticker:** My Mind's Eye ● **Brads:** AC ● **Font:** AL Heavenly ● **Paper:** K&Co. ● **Scalloped card:** Waste Not Paper ● **Sequins:** Papier Valise ● **Tag:** Cavallini & Co.

SEQUIN TAG SET By Renee

CREATE FLOWERS and other tag accents from a collection of sequins. Machine stitch for added interest.

Font: My Type of Font ● **Sequins and pipe cleaner:** Westrim ● **Stamps:** Hero Arts ● **Tab:** AL

By Jamie
LOVE YOU

Cut several circles from assorted patterned papers. Cut tulle into a circle; secure to layout with brads and gems. Layer photos and papers. Print journaling onto a transparency, then stamp an image underneath with paint. Staple to page. Add fabric tag, domino, etc. for embellishments.

Domino: Boxer ● **Fabric tag:** Scrapworks and 7g ● **Font:** AL Old Remington and 2Peas Miss Happy ● **Paper:** Hambly, CI, MAMBI and My Mind's Eye ● **Stamp:** Michaels

NEW NIECE
By Leslie

Mat photo on chipboard. Wrap tulle around one side and attach at the back of the photo. Tie a piece of ribbon in center of tulle wrap. Adhere embellished photo to page. Finish rest of layout with ribbon, lace, printed transparency and a clay "A" for the initial. Cut journaling into a circle and frame with a silver ring.

Flowers: Kaleidoscope ● **Font:** AL Tia A Capital Idea ● **Lace and ribbon:** MM ● **Paper:** BG and Chatterbox ● **Transparencies:** AL

WAITING

By Renee

Create a background of layered tulle squares attached to a pale cardstock. On title block, accent with a rolled piece of tulle secured with a decorative brad. Add hand stitches here and there.

Brad: AL ● **Fonts:** Paquita, KarrotHmk, Jailbird Jenna, AL Fat Boy, CA Fusion, Champignon, CA Scribb, My Type of Font, CherylsHand and Antique-Olive ● **Tulle:** Joann's ● **Waxed linen:** Paper Moon

THREE

By Cathy

STITCH MANY layers of white and pink tulle to layout. Apply letter sticker and stitch over the top numerous times.

Font: Slurry ●
Stickers: MM

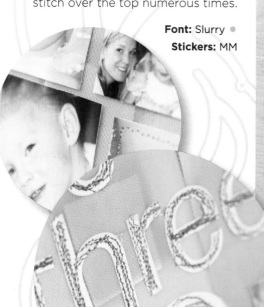

IN A graphics or photo-editing program, create two 12" wide text boxes, one with teal fill and one with black. Add title and journaling in white/ clear and colored text; print. Add paper strips, punched circles, tags and brads.

HANDSOME

By Lisa

Back in junior high, he was the dorky, overweight kid with the bottle-thick glasses. The class clown, as it were. ● But look at him now. He's one of those guys who will only get better looking the older he gets. Jerk. And he's just about perfect in every other way, too. He can build anything, fix anything, do anything. He's athletic and takes care of himself, he's a good dad. Sheesh! ● I sometimes think I won the husband lottery. But it's not always easy being married to Mr. Perfect. I'm not an insecure person by nature, but it's hard sometimes...the doubts creep in. I wonder what he sees in me. I don't like thinking that way, so I push those thoughts away quickly. ● We've been married almost 12 years. A long time. Been through some rough stuff, too - infertility ain't a party, you know? But we're doing just fine. We don't fight - although I think that's partly because he'd rather give in on something than get into it with me. Can't blame him there, can I? We're not overly affectionate with each other, but we have our own "love currency," as my friend Margie puts it. We show our love for each other in different ways. ● As a bonus, he makes really cute babies. So I think I'll keep him. My very handsome husband.

fyi: he wasn't always this handsome

Brads: AC ● **Fonts:** PMN Caecelia, Arial Black and 3 The Hard Way ● **Paper:** BG and My Mind's Eye

---

PA

By Robyn

Measure the distance for the brads so they are equal. Tape the thread on the backside of the layout and lay across the front. Punch small holes on each side of the thread and add brad on top so it holds the thread in place. Continue to do this to create the argyle pattern.

Brads, paper and ribbon: MM ● **Chipboard letters:** Rusty Pickle ● **Pen:** Stampin' Up! ● **Photo corner:** Advantus ● **Stamp:** Hero Arts

WOOF

By Leslie

For the border strips, cut ⅞" strips of chipboard and stitch down each side. Crinkle for a rugged look. Place on each side of the journaling and add brads for a decorative border.

Font: Amer Type Cnd • **Mesh and frame:** MM • **Paper:** K&Co., SEI and Cherry Arte • **Tie tack brads:** AL • **WOOF dog tag/charm:** Flair Design

Having a dog... It is life changing! We never knew we even wanted a dog until we saw this lil' guy... we have always been "cat people". It has been a shock to our system realizing how much work a dog is. It has taken more love & patience than I thought we had in us. I will admit that some days it is really hard juggling a pup & two young children. But... with Henry, his unconditional love is a constant force in our home. I know how lucky we are to know the love of this dog. For him, the work's totally worth the reward!

By Jennifer

BRIGHTEN

With a pencil, sketch rays coming from a circular photo. Poke holes in a pattern along lines. Erase lines and add brads through holes. Rub-on name onto large brads.

Brads: MM, AC, Accent Depot and Karen Foster • **Font:** Splendid • **Rub-ons:** AL

By Gillian AIM 4 HAPPY

USE CHARMS within title to represent a word. Attach charms to layout by inserting a brad from the back of the layout and bend the prongs over the loops.

Brads: Doodlebug Designs • **Charms:** Around the Block • **Stickers:** AC

With 3 kids, each approximately 2 years apart from the next, we've had our share of tantrums. Still do. Probably still will for a number of years. I know it's kind of your job as young children to be ornery little beasties sometimes. I accept that. But boy howdy, you're GOOD at your job. I mean, you bring real talent to the tantrum table. It's interesting to see how differently you each express your anger. Kyle, you prefer the silent, moody style. You've got a great glare, and you're not afraid to use it. Sean, there's really nothing silent about you, much less your tantrums. Your decibel levels are impressive, to say the least. Emma. Wow. You've taken Sean's pension for cacophony and ran with it. You add to the mix, however, that shrieking, glass-shattering frequency that only little girls seem to be able to produce. (Y-Chromosome Carriers need not attempt it. Sorry, fellas...you're just not equipped.) It's a well-balanced combo, I suppose. But you short people need to understand something. That old adage, "If Mama ain't happy, ain't nobody happy"? Yeah. It's got some real merit. Consider it. 'Cause you're harshin' my mellow, man.

written June. 2006 ; current ages: 7, 5 and 3

OUT WITH THE GIRLS

By Patricia

Layer several papers for background. Adhere photos. Attach charms to punched circles. Cut some title letters from cardstock and ink the edges. Cut the other letters from felt, hand stitch and adhere to layout.

Charms: Accent Factory, Westrim and Beader's Paradise • **Font:** AL Constitution and AL Uncle Charles • **Paper:** The Paper Company and AL • **Waxy Flax:** SW

saturday out with the

Sometimes I feel like I spend so much time with my children that I am rarely around adults for much time. Luckily, I have a great group of friends who go out once in a while. We are all busy and it can be a challenge to find a time that works for all of us, but we always have a great time when we do. This Saturday we went to the White House Cafe for breakfast. It was wonderful. Clover ranted about this place and she was right. It had charm and character, and the food was delicious. We went purse shopping and caught a chick-flick after that. It was just what I needed! Clover, Cassie, Stephanie, and me—June 3, 2006

By Jennifer
SO CHARMING

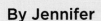reate circle accents with paper and stitching. Add charms with small stitches.

Charms: Blue Moon • **Fonts:** AL Meaningful and WinterthurCondensed • **Paper:** Scenic Route, K&Co., Paper Fever, Chatterbox and Anna Griffin • **Die cut:** Cricut, Provo Craft

My mother-in-law is the most thoughtful gift-giver I know. Gifts from her are always extra special and are sure to bring a smile to your face. A few years back for Christmas, she gave me a charm bracelet and a single Noel charm from my favorite jeweler, James Avery. Since then, she has added charms for various holidays and occasions. My sweet brother, who is also great with gifts, has given me a few, too. This bracelet means a lot to me and I adore wearing it. So charming. {2006}

Monogram - from Mike.

Two girls - because of Kay & Audrey.

Flip flop - due to my love of St. John.

Two hearts - from when we got married.

Roxie bone - from Mike.

Mother's heart - when Colin was born.

Bible - another faith reminder.

Angel - with Colin's b-day, from Mike.

Cross heart - reminder of my faith.

Noel - my first charm.

Special DIL - my favorite... so special.

"M" heart - from Mike.

BASKETBALL
By Cathy

Apply acrylic paint to a basketball and roll it over sections of the layout. Color in the seams with pencil. Adhere title, journaling and photos; embellish with hand stitching.

Font: Broken Wing • **Paper:** BG • **Stickers:** Sandylion

By Candice
WHIMSICAL

Using a pencil, draw paisley shapes and the word "Whimsical" in the bottom left corner of the page. Using a paper piercer, poke holes, then hand embroider. Repeat for the star burst designs, border and the word "little" at the top of the page. Add crystals and flower gems. Adhere journaling cut into strips.

Flower gems: Wal-Mart

By Mellette

B&M

Print large ampersand on white cardstock and cut out to use as a template. Turn ampersand to the back and place on yellow cardstock; trace around sign. Use a paper piercer to poke holes along the markings. Turn yellow cardstock over to front. Hand embroider the design by using a satin stitch and embroidery floss. Embroider on tags to use for the title.

Button: AL • **Definitions sticker, clips, paper flower, ribbon attachment, brads and gem stickers:** MM • **Paper:** Cross My Heart, MM, DCWV and Prism • **Ribbon:** Michaels and MM • **Rub-ons:** AL and CI

JUMP
By Kelli

CUT WAVES from cardstock. Adhere strips of patterned paper to the wave. Trim edges; layer the waves on the page and stitch along the edges.

Paper: AL, KI, Chatterbox, Kaleidoscope, Scenic Route, Pressed Petals, Sweetwater, BG and EK Success • **Pen:** Pigment Pro

PERFECT SUMMER PLAYDATE

By Lisa

PRINT NUMBERS on background cardstock, setting the type color to a light gray. Print text over the numbers. Add strips of patterned papers and file folder labels. Add photos and tags.

Fonts: Century Schoolbook, Bookman Old Style, ITC American Typewriter, Blackjack and Copperplate Gothic Bold. • **Labels:** Avery • **Paper:** BG and My Mind's Eye

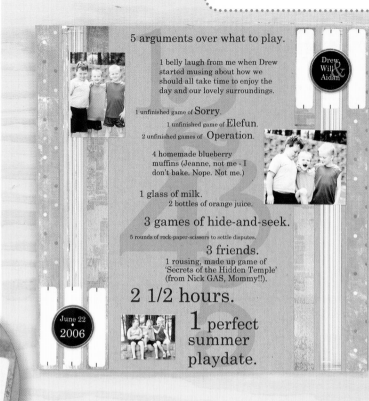

5 arguments over what to play.

1 belly laugh from me when Drew started musing about how we should all take time to enjoy the day and our lovely surroundings.

1 unfinished game of Sorry.

1 unfinished game of Elefun.

2 unfinished games of Operation.

4 homemade blueberry muffins (Jeanne, not me - I don't bake. Nope. Not me.)

1 glass of milk.

2 bottles of orange juice.

3 games of hide-and-seek.

5 rounds of rock-paper-scissors to settle disputes.

3 friends.

1 rousing, made up game of 'Secrets of the Hidden Temple' (from Nick GAS, Mommy!!).

2 1/2 hours.

1 perfect summer playdate.

June 22 2006

Drew, Will & Aidan

YOU TOOK THIS PHOTO

By Danielle

CUT STATIONERY labels in half and layer across page. Rubber stamp over the top.

Gaffer tape: 7gypsies • **Labels and stickers:** Cavallini & Co. • **Paper:** Rouge de Garance and Li'l Davis • **Rub-ons:** AL • **Stamps:** Fontwerks and Inkadinkado • **Stickers:** MM

Brads: SEI ●
**Chipboard,
silhouette and photo
corners:** Advantus
● **Paper:** Lasting
Impressions ●
Photo turn: 7gypsies
● **Sticker:** MM

R&R
By Robyn

A ffix four strips
of labels
together to
create a square. Add
strips of cardstock
and photo around the
labels. Stitch numerous
lines across the page.
Brush glitter glue onto
raw chipboard letters.

THE BOYS
By Jamie

A dhere matted photos
to background.
Arrange label
stickers and
hand write
journaling.
Add strips
of patterned
papers and
rub-ons.

Label and epoxy:
Li'l Davis ● **Paper:**
Kaleidoscope and
Hambly ● **Rub-ons:** AL and CI ●
Stamps: Hero Arts ● **Transparent letters:** KI

BOOKMARKS

By Jennifer

Add text to photos in Photoshop. Print and assemble with cardstock and sewing machine. Add ribbons and paper flowers with stitching. Create pocket with message.

Flowers: Prima • **Fonts:** Winterthur-Condensed, LittleDays, Inkster, Blue Highway Condensed and AL Slab • **Ribbon:** May Arts, Offray and MM

By Danielle SWEET TART

TO MAKE the flowers, cut abstract shapes from felt and chenille. Add hand stitching along with buttons and oil pastels.

Buttons and rub-ons: AL • **Font:** AL Old Remington • **Stamps:** Fontwerks

BABY GIRL

By Patricia

To make the flowers, paint chipboard shapes; embellish with bits of patterned paper, smaller chipboard shapes, buttons and the title cut into a circle. Mount journaling block with photo and chipboard flowers to white card-stock. Outline the flowers with doodles and cut out. Adhere entire piece to patterned paper background.

Chipboard shapes: Fancy Pants and KI • **Fonts:** AL Uncle Charles and AL Constitution • **Paper:** AL

ENDLESS SUMMER

By Ashley

Create flowers from tags, round embellishments and small flower accents. Layer some pieces to create flowers, add buttons and brads to centers, then adhere to page. For the stems, use twill, thin strips of metal mesh or hand stitches. Hand stitch title, add flower brads set with rhinestones and add remainder of title in flowery rub-ons. Cut journaling into strips and place lines of journaling as stems, then top with small paper flowers.

Chipboard: Maya Road • **Epoxy sticker and twill:** AL • **Font:** Elephant • **Letters:** K&Co • **Metal mesh:** MM • **Paper:** MM and Anna Griffin • **Paper flowers:** Doodlebug Designs • **Rhinestones:** Westrim • **Rub-ons:** AL and BG • **Sequins:** Queen & Co. • **Stamp:** Purple Onion • **Tags:** AL, MM and Advantus • **Watchglass:** Scrapworks

LITTLE THINGS By Gillian

Use straight pins to "anchor" decorative elements to layout or use straight pins to represent letters in the title, such as the "I" used here.

Font: American Typewriter • **Stickers:** AC

It's the little things that get me. Probably because there are so very many of them. You are represented in every room of my home, in one way or another. In my life, every facet. So many little things, just waiting to remind me that you're gone. The other night as I threaded my sewing machine, it hit me that I wouldn't be able to call you in a sewing panic anymore. To have you talk me down from the edge when my bobbin is going haywire and my stitches are in knots. You were my crafts guru, always available for technical support and patient instructions. Ever the teacher, and happy to do it. I wish I'd have let you teach me to crochet. You assured me it was easy, but I just didn't want to take the time to learn something that, to me, looked so complicated. And so it is that the crochet hook you gave me last Christmas is tucked aside. Another little thing that I'll come across one day. And I know it will get me. The little things always do.

ART By Cathy

REDUCE AND print favorite pieces of child's art. Adhere to layout along with journaling. Embellish with quilter's pins and rub-ons.

Font: 2Peas Weathered Fence • **Paper and rub-ons:** BG • **Pins:** Blue Feather Products, Inc.

STEP OUT INTO SPRING

By Rhonda

Mount torn muslin to chipboard, then adhere to layout. Make sun accents with straight pins. Add small beads to some of the pins. Add ribbon and decorative tape to upper right corner of layout and secure using two pins.

Chipboard: WorldWin • **Die cuts:** SW • **Paper:** AL • **Stamp:** MM • **Stickers:** My Mind's Eye • **Tag:** K&Co.

COLOR

By Candice

Stick straight pins in wide rick-rack to create a border. Use small flowers and green ribbon to create flowers placed randomly in the border of pins. Apply rub-ons down left side of page for the title. Adhere journaling to a tag and affix under photo.

Flowers: Prima • **Paper:** Kaleidoscope • **Ribbon:** May Arts • **Rub-ons:** AC and BG • **Stamps:** Fontwerks

A FAMILY OF BUILDERS

By Margie

Paperclip: K&Co • **Twill, paper and bookplates:** BG

Frame small photos with a large bookplate. Turn another large bookplate into a frame for an accordion booklet. On the booklet, add homespun accents like fabric, ribbon, embroidery stitches, hand journaling and small photos. Attach the back page of the booklet to the background cardstock. Punch holes on either side of the bookplate and string twill through the holes. Tie the twill to keep the booklet closed.

By Leslie

ROMEO ROMEO

Arrange papers and photos on page. Journal with white text in an orange textbox. Hand cut hearts from paper and sew down centers. Add to page. Place bookplates on the layout and use a pencil to trace where to cut. Remove bookplates and cut a window behind each bookplate. Fasten bookplates over windows and add mesh to the back.

Bookplates and measuring tape: MM ◦ **Chipboard circles:** Imagination Projects ◦ **Font:** Serifa BT ◦ **Metal bar:** 7gypsies ◦ **Paper:** Scenic Route, 7gypsies and K&Co.

By Jackie **LUCKY**

CREATE THE background with several different papers cut into blocks and trace a CD for a couple of half circles. Place photo and stickers letters. Then arrange a bunch of bookplates filled with journaling, small flowers, a map, fabric, tiny photos, patterned papers, etc. Finish off with fasteners on some of the bookplates.

Bookplates: MM and KI ◦ **Chipboard arrow:** KI ◦ **Chipboard date:** Li'l Davis ◦ **Flowers:** Prima ◦ **Papers:** AL, K&Co., EK Success and Doodlebug Designs ◦ **Ribbon:** May Arts ◦ **Stickers:** AC

TELL US WHAT YOUR FAVORITE PAGE IS...